Save Your Life

Rashidah Id-Deen

Autobiography of a Woman's Extraordinary Spiritual Journey
from Survivor of Assaults to Leader,
and Contemporary Guide for Survivors of Assault

Save Your Life

Copyright © 2011 by
Rashidah Id-Deen

All rights reserved: No part of this book may be reprinted or reproduced without permission from the author, Rashidah Id-Deen, with the exception of brief excerpts for book reviews.

All print, CD, or DVD rights related to this book belong to the author. For information regarding permission to reproduce selections from this book, write to Ms. Id-Deen at
2525 Welsh Road, Suite J1
Philadelphia, Pennsylvania 19114
or
justproportionsfoundation@yahoo.com.

ISBN 978-0-615-55309-2

PorterVision Multimedia, Inc.
4848 Lemmon Avenue, Suite 606
Dallas, Texas 75219

Dedicated

*to my children ~
Ayesha, Rahjan, Nadiyah,
Rasul, Qasim & Amani*

*to every woman struggling for sanity
in an insane world,
struggling for power and dignity
in a world where men rule and can be like feral animals*

*to spiritually enlightened women and men everywhere
who insist on spreading blessings, light and love*

Acknowledgments

First, I want to thank the Almighty Creator. Without Him nothing is possible and with Him everything is possible.

To my mother and father, Kalimah A. and Waheed A. Rahmaan, thank you for your unconditional love, support and guidance. To my sister, Sakinah, and brother, Tariq, thank you both for showing me the value of being true to yourself.

To my six children: Ayesha, Rahjan, Nadiyah, Rasul, Qasim and Amani, thank each of you for showing me a new and different personality, facet and layer of my spiritual being. I am honored to be your mother. To my grandchildren and great-grandson, all of you continue to elevate and evolve my life and I am grateful to experience the journey.

To Eddie Currie, thank you for being the ultimate friend during a time when it would have been easy to leave me feeling friendless. You made yourself accessible during the two trials it took to get a standing conviction of the rapist posing as an upstanding doctor. He had made the lives of many women hell. We finally put him behind bars. In your firefighting career, you saved lives. As a friend, you saved mine.

To Jamil Abdul Malik, thank you for expanding my awareness and definition of love to that of a more spiritual relationship and proving to me that I could love outside the box. Despite circumstances, challenges and people, I learned with you the power of love and how to harness, respect, and sacrifice for it.

To Cynthia Jackson, thank you for believing in me when I did not feel it would ever be possible to believe in myself. You remain a blessing in my life.

To Sabreen, thank you for your poem, *Rashidah or the word Beautiful*. It reclaimed something that had been stolen from me and returned it home to my soul.

To Bishop Ricky Gordon and Mrs. Jacque Gordon, your family, and the church family of Wise Fisherman Church of Dallas, thank you for your unconditional support of my cause and vision for my organization, Just Proportions, when others in my own community did not provide these. Thank you for bringing awareness of my organization not only within your own church, but in other religious places of worship. You encouraged many to listen to my testimony.

Lady Jacque, you are indeed an amazing example of faith, womanhood, motherhood and sisterhood. You are the total beautiful package inside and out. Bishop, thank you for your consistent honesty and authenticity as a pastor and man of substance. Bishop and Lady Jacque, thank you and your wonderful children for being "Wise Fishermen" to both my daughter, Amani, and I.

To Debra A. Porter (aka Lady "D"), you are the epitome of the phenomenal woman and friend I aspire to be. You are my dear sister and kindred spirit and I will forever remain grateful for our friendship and sisterhood. Thank you for your encouraging and supportive words of healing every time we speak. You are medicine for my soul. Not only do I love you, I admire you. May we always rise together!

Love & Blessings!
Rashidah

*You are beautiful
and it does not matter
that some foul intentioned demon
soiled that word for you*

*Whispered it in your ear
and made you recoil from it
hid it beneath his intentions
till the act of violation
became synonymous with it*

*I'll take it back for you
I'll take it back, Rashidah
because you are beautiful
You Are*

*(Excerpt from the poem,
"Rashidah or the word Beautiful"
by Sabreen Abdal-Razzaaq El)*

Save Your Life

Not Your Image

Contents

Foreword	*xvii*
Introduction	*xxi*
Innocent, but no Longer Pure	23
Why Me?	29
Fast Forward~	
Young Wife and Mother of Five	30
A Husband's Plea: Forgive Me,	
Take Care of my Babies	33
Living for My Children	37
Life Goes On	39
First Trial	46
A New Start in Texas	50
Newsworthy from the Heart of Texas	52
P#428324	57
The Year 2005~	
New Trial	58
Some Special Childhood Memories, Too	62
Letter to My Children	65
The Power of Self~Love	70
Just Proportions Foundation	
and Collaborations	72
Contemporary Guide for	
Survivors of Assault Introduction	74
Part 1: Knowledge is Power	76
Part 2: Save Your Life Worksheet	
Preparation;	
Save Your Life Worksheet	84

Part 3: My Space~Celebration of My Life   95
Part 4: Directory for Counseling
         and Referral Services   97
Just Proportions Privilege   103
Appendix

Foreword

Rashidah Id-Deen, Founder of Just Proportions Foundation for survivors of sexual assault and domestic abuse, discovered that when your life and sanity are threatened and nobody else charges in to save you, you must save yourself.

Rashidah was a beautiful child, dutiful and respectful. Many were proud of the image she projected for herself, family, and community. As a preteen, she had a rosy picture of her future life as the perfect woman, wife and mother. At age twelve, that picture-perfect image was shattered.

Rashidah was raped.

As survivor of this assault, another in her late forties, and domestic violence throughout many of her adult years, Rashidah saw that what was expected of her was silence and strength: silence about the violations, and demonstrations of strength in the face of adversities. In other words, she was expected to present an image of perfection that was a total denial of the pain in her reality.

She created a personal *cover girl* ideal of feminine fitness and beauty, emulating 1960s fashion models in her favorite magazines. The models seemed to live in a world that was beyond human suffering.

Eventually, Rashidah became a professional fitness instructor. Public success belied her private feelings of failure.

It was after being sexually assaulted in her forties by a licensed sports therapist that Rashidah developed an authentic strength based on her reality, not an image. She took the rapist to trial. Actually, it took two trials to finally convict him.

She won!

The rapist was sentenced to seven years in a state prison. He lost his license to practice physical therapy ever again, and was subjected to placement on a sexual offenders' registry for a minimum of twenty years.

The trials were grueling, but whatever does not kill us makes us stronger. Rashidah embraced a spiritual journey, relinquished her false images of perfection, and welcomed her new reality-based strength.

Her spiritual consciousness produced a desire to help others, and Just Proportions Foundation was born. She is Founder and Director of the 501 (c)(3) non-profit foundation.

"When our lives are in just proportions," she teaches, "we live in balance. When we live in balance, we manifest wellness and recover quickly after suffering illnesses, diseases, or life injustices."

Yes, Rashidah learned what all of us must: when nobody charges in to save us, we must save ourselves.

Debra A. Porter, Founder
PorterVision Multimedia, Incorporated

Introduction

This book is long overdue. I write it as a voice for every woman who has donned a too-perfect smile to stop close inspection of her soiled self-esteem or beaten body. I write it for every woman who has dressed to the nines and held her head high to costume evidence of violations inflicted on her body, mind and soul.

It is time to save our lives, not the images resembling perfection that we show to the world to hide our pain. It is time!

This book is truth, my truth. Prepare because parts of it are ugly: I document evil, specifically the evil of sexual assault.

We won't often hear about this evil in our religious places where we worship, or hear it called out and chastised. We won't hear it often in our homes, denounced at the dinner table; but we should.

Our children need to know that in addition to love, joy, and security, there is evil in the world. It can walk on two legs and call itself friend or family.

This book also serves as a guide for women who are struggling to survive abuse. Women are expected to be tender and tough at the same time: tender as lover or wife, tough as human shield and shelter for our children.

With this forced merger of opposites, it is no wonder we sometimes feel schizophrenic, hearing voices from our past and present pulling us in diverse directions. Add to these challenging expectations, dynamics of abuse and the greatest miracle is that we survive our traumas and dramas.

I want all my sisters to know that claiming our voices is about empowerment. I am not whining and complaining. I am giving notice for those of us who have had enough of abuse.

"We who have been raped, beaten, or profaned won't take it anymore!"

Now that these truths have been pronounced, I will take you on a journey in time to show you how I arrived at this moment of power. We will start with a young girl's innocence right before she discovered powerlessness. I was this child.

Rashidah Id-Deen

Innocent, but no Longer Pure

I remember being excited on that Monday, July 11, 1966, because it was my father's birthday. I was 12. It was a joyous day; I could finally use the money that I earned from summer babysitting to buy him a gift. That was a proud moment for me.

The weather forecast was for a high of 95 degrees. I remember waking up early that morning, and rushing to my closet to check out the fashionable dresses, skirts, and blouses crowding my closet. I pictured the stylish models in Ebony magazine. That special day, I would do my best to look just like them.

I had a lot of frilly–very feminine–clothes that I always accessorized with bows and whatnot. But there was this particular dress I wore all the time (smiles) because it was my favorite! I felt so grown up in it.

The dress was brown and beige, all nice and soft with a cotton feel to it. Brown and beige, like me. When I wore it, I would spin around in a circle and my dress twirled with me. It made me look like a young woman, not a child.

That morning, when my mother came to my room, I was already dressed, and spinning.

"Rashidah, why always that dress?" Mama sometimes had a unique way of frowning and smiling at the same time.

"It makes me feel all grown up," I beamed.

She shook her head. Mama loved seeing me happy, but hated seeing her little girl grow up so fast. She knew what I did not, yet: the world can be awfully cold and cruel for a woman; but maybe, just maybe she could spare her baby girl–at least for a while.

"Rashidah! Stop trying to grow up so fast!"

I managed to stop twirling under Mama's watchful eye. There were other fun things to do.

I delighted in experimenting with new hairstyles and current fashion trends, like those in magazines. It used to drive my parents crazy. Daddy would have been happy with me in braids, ribbons, and bows forever, which is how my grandma Eula always styled my hair.

I also reveled in listening to music–mature music. Jazz and R&B were staples in our household. So were books.

Fantasizing was another fun thing to do. I *loved* imagining myself as a future woman, wife and mother. I wanted to be the best, as all three.

I was both a little girl and a budding young woman. Music, books, fashion and fantasies transported me into a realm of grown-up consciousness, a grown-up world with feelings that were foreign to the child in me, yet intriguing.

Finally, it was time for me to go babysit. I almost ran down the street to the children's apartment, by myself. Back then in the 60s, growing up, there were no worries about people abducting children, or someone

Save Your Life

being a pedophile, or anything like that. It was a safe place to be growing up–so I thought–in Newark, NJ.

I had been working as a babysitter, caring for three precious children, two toddlers and a baby. My parents knew the parents. So, we felt safe with my repeated visits.

The babies were napping in their bedroom. I had fed them. So far, so good. My parents would have been proud of me. I was proud of me; it was time for a little reward.

Remember, music was an important part of my life. I put a 45 black vinyl record on the turntable in the living room. It played 33s, 45s, and 78s. Remember them?

The record on the turntable was my favorite: "Face It, Girl, It's Over" by the fabulous Ms. Nancy Wilson. It was number fifteen on the US R&B chart.

I was singing in the bathroom, restyling my hair for the nth time, and beaming at my reflection in the mirror. I was in a picture-perfect little world: a calm before the storm.

He came home early: the children's father called out for me from the living room.

"Rashidah!"

"Hi!" My voice must have sounded so young and innocent. "I wasn't expecting you home so soon," I said. "Is anything wrong?"

He was sitting on the sofa. He patted a space on it near him.

"I'm not feeling well, Rashidah."

Rashidah Id-Deen

The children's father reached for me. "Come on over here," he said, "sit next to me." His voice was authoritative.

Now, I was raised to mind my elders. I thought nothing of following his orders. Grown-ups protected you, right?

He took one of my hands, guiding me to the sofa to sit beside him.

"You're such a pretty girl." He smiled.

I know now that I was staring into the face of danger.

Then, there was no way I could presage the end of an era of my life, an era of innocence.

This was before the proliferation of daytime Talk-show TV with live interviews from rapists in prison. This was a pre-Oprah time, before home audiences viewed packaged wisdom dispensed between commercials.

"Thank you," I answered. My home-training demanded my politeness.

What came next was beyond anything in a child's book of etiquette. His grown man's fingers started caressing, and trailing up and down my arms.

Though naïve, I knew something was so wrong.

"No!" I tried to pull away, but could not get away from his groping hands.

"Please..." I begged, still not wanting to believe this.

Of course, he just got bolder, hearing my plea.

Save Your Life

"Rashidah!"

He ripped my beautiful brown and beige dress–brown and beige like me–off my shoulder.

"Stop!" I cried. "What are you doing?"

A hard, clawing hand under my dress, prying open my locked legs, answered me.

I wept.

The children's father was now my monster. I wondered how in heaven he could…

He disgusted me…prying open my cramping thighs, sucking on my aching, bruised breasts…

I was living a nightmare that only got worse.

I remember one moment more vividly than all others that day: the sharp, *ripping pain* as he stabbed my vagina with his penis. I was a virgin.

He was mean and vicious. I knew then–he had planned this.

I fought with all my strength.

The more I fought to re-clamp my legs, the more vicious he got.

Can't he tell that I'm locked? I kept thinking. *I'm locked.*

That human piece of filth broke the lock.

Do you remember the record? It was set to repeat.

Face it, girl… It's over, girl… played over and over. It was as if this song–once my favorite–was telling me, telling *me*, something.

Rashidah Id-Deen

My purity was over. Innocence? Over.

My mind was overwhelmed with pain, fear, and confusion. Eventually, a mental fugue spared me from what seemed like a never-ending nightmare.

I cannot tell you where the children were while their babysitter was being violated–by their dad. If they were still safely sleeping, I wish I had been with them. I wish his wife had come home.

Telling my parents was the next nightmare. They were devastated, angry, shocked, ashamed…all of the above…all on Dad's birthday. What a hell of a birthday present.

On July 11, 1966, I started the day as a young girl full of joy and hope. By day's end, I was traumatized, and that trauma would shadow me the rest of my life.

Eventually, my dad and an uncle ran the child rapist out of town. Then, my loving family did what they thought was best for me. They modeled silence and strength.

Why Me?

When a woman, girl, man or boy is violated, "Why me?" is the question that might torment her or him for weeks, months, or sometimes years. Many counselors recognize it as part of the Grief stage of Anger.

When I was raped, I grieved the loss of my "self." The Rashidah I knew was dead. The innocent, secure reality I knew departed.

Five stages of Grief have been widely discussed by counselors and mental health caregivers. They are Denial, Anger, Bargaining, Depression and Acceptance. It is my understanding that these stages were initially applied to people suffering terminal illnesses. Later, they were applied to anyone experiencing catastrophic loss.

I have had decades to ask myself, "Why me?"

My answers are these: The man was filth. The man was evil.

Undoubtedly, some of you will tout the virtue of forgiveness. I understand your view. Forgiveness can be a mercy; but, I wonder *where was his mercy for a twelve-year-old girl*?

In some societies, he would have been stoned to death. Unfortunately, I found myself asking again, "Why me?" in my adult life, when I suffered abuse in a marriage, and was sexually assaulted once more by someone I trusted.

Fast Forward~
Young Wife and Mother of Five

I have been married a few times. As a young girl, I had aspired to be the perfect woman, wife and mother.

My first husband, Rasul, was strong and bold, macho before Americans adopted the word and made it our own. He was also a young man with charm that was like magic. He could and did entice women, all ages and races.

For me, his power was the greatest lure. I was looking for the man who would shield me–keep me safe from evil, especially the kind that walked on two legs.

We were both eighteen when we married. By the age of twenty-five, I had five beautiful children with Rasul: Ayesha, Rahjan, Nadiyah, Rasul, Jr., and Qasim. We were married for fifteen years.

Rasul was my husband, lover, and the man I had hand-picked to secure my protection. He had a history of violence. I knew this. It just convinced me: he was the one strong enough to protect me.

What I did not know was that I would need to be protected from him.

He beat me physically, mentally, and emotionally throughout the marriage. He violated my trust, yet I loved him.

My children sometimes witnessed assaults of their mother. They witnessed my pain and powerlessness.

Save Your Life

My husband had been verbally and emotionally abused, as a child, by his mother. He felt ugly and unwanted. Before he abused me, I saw him as the most attractive man on earth, and he was very wanted by me.

One day, I needed a reprieve from abuse and a chance to take my beautiful children on an outing. They deserved something special.

I dressed all of them and off we went on an adventure–headed to downtown Newark. We were so excited, and I felt proud as I admired each one of my babies, and myself for being their mother.

I soon learned that not everyone would appreciate my pride. I was getting on a bus with my five. The sixth was not yet born. It never occurred to me that others would disapprove of my choice to have a large family. Public disapproval hit me like a ton of bricks.

The bus driver opened the door and we piled on board. Instantly, I caught the quizzical look on his face, not a smiling welcome. In front of his passengers, who were gawking, he loudly asked, "Is this a daycare!?"

I was completely thrown by his question-slash-comment; then, I decided that he was joking. Too soon, I realized he was not, and I noticed that several of the passengers were waiting with him for my answer. Their faces were judgment masks.

Indignantly and proudly, I answered, "NO, this isn't a daycare. These are all my children."

Rashidah Id-Deen

The sneers from the bus driver and passengers filled me with their potent sense of disapproval, although I was a married woman. I had never encountered such a direct confrontation regarding the number of children I chose to bring into the world.

I was aware that not many women by the age of twenty-five had five children. Still, never could I have anticipated such shocked and critical attitudes about my choice to be a young mother of five.

I did not let this censure stop me from treating my children to a special day; but, I never forgot this scalding public reproach.

A Husband's Plea:
Forgive Me, Take Care of my Babies

In my marriage with Rasul, shockwaves were coming that would not only hit me, but devastate the children that we both adored.

I knew before we married that Rasul was violent; but I never dreamed that he would rain down his rage on me. He could be so romantically charming, like a hero stepping straight out of a novel, declaring his devotion.

Something was fueling a mercurial moodiness in Rasul. I found out what that something was.

He was an intravenous drug user. My hero was an addict.

How could I not have known this before saying, *I do*? I was truly naïve.

Today, alarms would go off in my head that would deafen me.

Back then, I was clueless.

Drugs were part of Rasul's world. They were not part of mine. I knew some people got hooked on drugs, like heroin or cocaine. Some drank too much and became alcoholics. Politicians inundated airwaves with war on drugs rhetoric. This was usually to secure their two or four more years.

In the 1980s, an epidemic other than news-featured drug addiction hit America. A disease was spreading: it seemed that immune systems of people previously considered healthy were shutting down.

The press finally headlined the name for it, one already known by a select group of health scientists and physicians: AIDS. It is an acronym for Acquired Immune Deficiency Syndrome.

We learned that AIDS is a complex of illnesses and symptoms that overwhelm a body when the immune system is weakened by the Human Immunodeficiency Virus, also known as HIV. The virus is transmitted through bodily fluids–blood, semen, vaginal secretions, breast milk–and intravenous drug use is a high-risk behavior for transmitting HIV, along with unprotected sex.

Rasul got very sick. We had no idea what was wrong with him. I was sure that whatever it was, he would get over it. I was wrong.

Rasul was diagnosed with AIDS, which at that time was a death sentence. The day he found out, I was at his side. Seeing pain and fear in his eyes–my rock of a man–was almost unbearable.

He was hospitalized in 1987, and would never leave. From that day forward, his decline was quick. Rasul's body weight plummeted; he was soon half his previous size.

AIDS awareness was new, then, and misinformation was prevalent. Even doctors and nurses were fearful of people with the diagnosis. Often, immune-compromised patients were medically treated with a lamentable lack of compassion.

Visitors were required to "mask up." Some scientists theorized that AIDS might be airborne.

I refused to "mask up." I told Rasul and his medical caregivers that I had slept with and shared intimacy with this man for fifteen years. At this point, it would serve me no purpose to shun him.

Rasul's mother and sister came to his hospital bedside. I know they loved him, but fear kept them at a distance. They never hugged or kissed him during their visits. This broke his heart, and mine as well.

My husband did not want our children to visit. He was ashamed because of the stigma of AIDS, and he feared that he would infect the very people he wanted to protect more than any in this world, his children.

Most of his final days in the hospital, Rasul was alone, except for me.

One day, when he obviously felt too weak to even lift his head, I climbed into his bed to comfort him. He melted in my arms as I drew him close. Rasul's body was frail, notably missing his pre-illness muscles.

His hair had not been brushed in…I could not remember how long, so I began to brush it. My husband's huge smile was a reward. I was soothing him, and in a way comforting myself.

I hugged and kissed Rasul, and told him he would always have my love. The affection that I saw in his face at that moment had been gone for so long. I welcomed it.

I refused to let this man die without a fight. Despite years of suffering abuse at his hands, I did not want him to leave this world without feeling my love.

I told Rasul that this could be his wake-up call. He could make his life right with God.

Because he could not or would not talk much during his final days, I spent most of our hospitalized time together reading to my husband from the Holy Qur'an. Finally, when Rasul spoke to me, after days of hearing nothing from him, he delivered words I never knew I had longed to hear.

"Rashidah…you're a *great* mother."

We cried.

I believe this was my husband's way of saying, "Forgive me," though he never said these words.

"Please…always," his voice was raspy and his speech was slow, "take care of my babies. You've always been a great mom. Take care of my babies."

I was holding one of his frail hands, hands which had once been so strong, when a frightening alarm went off. It was Rasul's heart monitor.

"No!" My mind was screaming, pleading for him to hold on, "No, you can't leave me." But my husband did not hold on.

Rasul had cardiac arrest. At the age of thirty-two, the father of my five children left this world, right before my eyes.

Living for My Children

I felt as if I were sinking in quicksand. Rasul was dead. I was a young widow with children. Oh, and my oldest child, my fifteen-year-old daughter, had just made me a grandmother.

Quicksand.

I grieved, I wept, I wanted to die…but I had my children who needed me.

It was a very dark and scary time in my life. Not only had I become the sole head of my household, I now had five devastated children grappling with grief's anger and depression.

So, when my husband's doctors recommended I get examined to see if I had AIDS…

Quicksand.

Thank God, all tests came back negative. I wanted to live.

I realized that despite my sorrows, God's mercy and grace have never forsaken me!

It was many years later that I shared with my children the true cause of their father's death. The AIDS stigma would have been too much for them to confront when they were younger.

My husband was buried in a cemetery that was right there in our neighborhood. For better or worse, he was still close.

One of my daughters would skip school and be found at the cemetery where he was buried. For my young family, the grief was torture.

We landed in family grief counseling. I sought individual therapy, additionally.

I was a Wreck.

Years of abuse had taken a tremendous toll on me.

Cynthia Jackson, a professional psychotherapist, became my saving grace. She saw qualities in me that I had not heard anyone attribute to me–strength of character that I never before allowed myself to recognize.

Though she was encouraging and motivational, Cynthia never allowed me to hide behind my pain. She helped me to merge that twelve-year-old little girl who was raped years ago with the woman, wife, and mother that I was and needed to be now.

Cynthia made me feel like a loved one, not a patient. I gratefully accepted her therapeutic interventions after my husband's death, and when another unbelievable trauma hit my life again. That quicksand feeling would return.

Life Goes On

During the years after I became a widow, I developed a new resilience, had to in order to survive. Vigorous feminine fitness and beauty were essential to my strong woman image and self-definition. I worked out for hours and made the YMCA a second home.

Still, the strength that most family and friends saw in me was what I sculpted to hide emotional scars. I battled with depression. Some days my spirits were high, and on others taxingly low.

God gave me a very unexpected gift during this time: another beautiful child, my sixth, a daughter.

Her name is Amani.

Yes, initially, I was in shock. I thought I was too old to have babies–I was a grandmother–and my other five were not happy when they found out I was pregnant.

Believe me when I say that I am understating their reactions, but life goes on...

I remarried. My second husband was the total opposite of my first. He never abused me during our ten years together, though our union had other challenges, as do most marriages. I was determined to never again be defined by a man's aggression. For self-protection, I became a marital aggressor.

I had not yet gained wisdom for living with just proportions. Some might refer to this as living in moderation or balance. Others might perceive just proportions as harmony. Counselors often speak of it as the wise use of boundaries.

Personal life experiences had skewed my view of the intricate relationship between a man and woman. In the dyad life script that was manifested in my world, someone got abused, usually the woman. Well, this time it was not going to be me.

I succeeded in keeping myself safe from physical abuse in my second marriage, but I was still haunted by the abuses of my past.

It is not a surprise that all that toxic stress produced medical illnesses.

In 1998, I developed agonizing arthritis with painful ankle inflammation. An acquaintance of mine at a YMCA referred me to a well-known sports doctor, who was highly credible.

I accepted the referral and started treatment, lymphatic drainage, to alleviate the swelling.

I put total faith in my reputable doctor.

He *raped* me.

How could...?!

How could this happen, again...?!

Pain, shame and powerlessness overwhelmed me.

I wanted to curl up and die right then, but could not.

I could not let this second rapist destroy me–destroy the Rashidah I had worked so hard to create and define.

In retrospect, I see that I had never fully recovered from my childhood rape or abuse suffered in my first marriage. This second sexual assault opened old wounds, and left new ones.

I had to live–I had to want to live. My children needed me. My marriage had already been falling apart, so I did not turn to my husband.

Thankfully, the Almighty Creator had given me Cynthia Jackson. I would eventually rely heavily on her, though I did not contact Cynthia immediately.

I was twice blessed when God sent another loyal, dynamic friend: Eddie Currie. He was a Plainfield, New Jersey firefighter.

Eddie and I used to workout at a YMCA every morning–he is not the one who referred me to the doctor-rapist–and consequently, we became very good friends. The refreshing thing about us was that we never had romantic interests. I was married and he was in a long-term relationship. Over time, we became acutely aware of one another's personalities and moods.

The sexual assault was on a Sunday.

I did my best to be Superwoman the following Monday.

I took my youngest child, Amani, to school: this was routine. Honestly, looking back I don't know how I managed to get through the night, get up the next day and continue on with my regimen.

I believe it was the only way I thought I could hold on to my sanity and a sense of the normal. When I was understandably flying out of control, I was looking for an anchor. I sought control in a routine that I could manage.

That post-assault morning, I was on a YMCA treadmill, as usual. Eddie did more than keep his workout pace. He immediately noticed that something was gravely wrong with his exercise partner; something was not right with my spirit.

Being a true friend, he wanted to know what was going on.

"Rashidah, what's wrong?"

I tried to lie.

"Nothing. I'm alright, Eddie. Got a lot on my mind."

He wasn't buying it. Through repeated conversations with Eddie days and weeks later, I learned that he picked up on body language that was flaring off me in waves.

After the workout that morning, Eddie refused to leave his wounded friend behind.

"Rashidah, let's meet up at my place where we can talk privately. Is that OK with you?"

Despite what had just happened with another man, I trusted Eddie Currie.

"Alright, Eddie." I needed a lifeline. "I'll meet you at your place."

In his home, I broke down.

"I was raped, last night."

Eddie's support and outrage on my behalf was that lifeline I needed. He was the first person I had told. I hadn't said a word to anyone else.

Save Your Life

"We've got to go the police, Rashidah."

Eddie was ready to do battle with me, but was gentle in insisting, "Don't let this guy get away with assaulting you."

He knew I was in shock. He knew I was hesitant because of the status of the rapist. Still, Eddie firmly, but respectfully urged me to seek justice–and I did.

Eddie Currie not only took me to the police station, he was with me every step of the way. When I spoke with a Rape Crisis counselor, he was there, even asked what he could do to help.

Though in a haze, I marveled. This man took action to save me. Never did he abandon, look down on, or criticize me.

In fact, during the trials–*yes, we took the doctor to trial*–this trusted friend was the most influential and credible corroborating witness I had. He gave valuable testimony, attested to my post-attack trauma.

I wish I could tell you that justice was swift, but it was not. It took years to get that rapist into court.

The long pre-trial era was agony.

I received death threats from his friends!

I was the one assaulted, yet I received death threats.

My car, my only transportation, was vandalized.

My family suffered. Watching me struggle to hold onto sanity almost pushed them over the edge.

Of course, more than one of my six children wanted to kill him. That only added to my stressors. The thought of any of my grown babies being jailed or imprisoned for murder kept me in a heightened state of anxiety for them and me.

I went to rape counseling, group and individual. Still, my psychological and physical health were deteriorating rapidly.

One day, while working out at the YMCA, I had a cardiac event. I was rushed to a hospital in an ambulance.

It was not a heart attack; but doctors warned me that I had serious heart problems, one of which was irregular heartbeats. This was due to the stress. A cardiologist placed me on nitroglycerin pills to prevent it.

It was a horrendous time. Newspaper reporters got wind of the story. A doctor accused of rape was just the kind of topic that could be sensationalized in the news.

As a result of the articles, three other women found the courage to step forth. The doctor had sexually assaulted them, too.

Of course, by the time the case was tried in 2003, only one other woman stood with me. I easily understood why the other two dropped out of the heated spotlight.

The emotional turmoil that a trial takes a woman through—it's hard to capture in words. You must face your attacker *and* convince twelve strangers that what you are telling them is the TRUTH. All the while you relive every aspect of it publicly in order to even have a chance of them believing you.

Save Your Life

So you are raped again, but this time publicly. This is why a lot of women will not file charges. You are re-victimized all over again. The perpetrators know this. They count on victims not filing charges.

We, who have been assaulted, deserve justice. We must fight on every level for our emotional and physical well-being. Not doing so only adds to our sense of defeat, depletion, shame and guilt.

It empowers us to expose and uphold the TRUTH by using any means necessary. It also sends a message to those who victimized us. They did not steal our souls.

Our souls belong only to GOD. With HIM, we will battle evil.

First Trial

I had seen countless television episodes with actors portraying slick lawyers and camera-ready clients, had read the latest legal suspense thrillers; but, this trial with all its impersonal legalese describing my personal agony was far worse than anything I had seen on TV.

I had moved away from New Jersey. It was no longer home–more on this later–but I insisted on returning to face the sexual offender-doctor.

In this chapter, I will try to capture the impersonal aspect of the proceedings, which became part of my very personal torture, as it was presented to the jury.

I identify myself here as RI. The man who assaulted me, I identify as Defendant, the defendant, or X.

STATE of New Jersey, Plaintiff-Respondent, v. X, Defendant-Appellant.

In 1997, RI suffered from rheumatoid arthritis. She testified that an acquaintance at a YMCA recommended she try therapy with the defendant, who specialized in massage therapy.

RI contacted Defendant. He told her that he worked at two locations, one was in his home located in Scotch Plains.

Save Your Life

RI arrived for the first massage. She met the defendant's wife and son, and completed medical forms. She reported feeling assured by meeting his family.

Before the massage therapy session, Defendant told RI that it was optional if she wanted to wear clothes during treatment. She chose to not wear them, she wanted the most effective professional treatment to alleviate pain.

Defendant left. RI undressed and positioned herself on the treatment table.

Defendant returned, performed massage therapy. RI reported that she could immediately feel positive effects.

Over a nine-month period, Defendant gave RI approximately ten massages. RI stopped therapy due to a decrease in funds. She informed Defendant that she would contact him when finances improved.

May 3, 1998: The defendant contacted RI, offered her a free massage. He described her as a loyal customer, despite her financial situation. She agreed to return and arrived at Defendant's home. No one else was present.

The routine massage came first. This was the expected treatment while she was on her back. When RI rotated onto her stomach, Defendant began performing deep pressure on her back with his forearm. He placed his knee on the table for more leverage. He had never done that before.

RI's face was in a headrest. She could not move.

Defendant told RI that he was going to apply more pressure.

Defendant then straddled her on the table with his knees at her thighs. Defendant's hand brushed against her vaginal area.

At first, RI assumed that it was accidental. However, Defendant continued to use his forearm to hold her still and leaned into her, inserting his fingers into her vagina and emitted a moaning sound.

Defendant asked, "How does this feel?"

RI could not speak or respond. Then Defendant stopped.

RI sat up on the table. Defendant began to talk with RI in a voice described as "monotone, almost ominous kind of voice."

Defendant told her that she could come over anytime for a massage. Because defendant would not leave the room, RI felt compelled to dress in front of him.

RI went up the stairs and walked quickly out the front door. RI raced to her car, got in and cried.

She drove around the corner and collapsed for several minutes. She drove to her parents' home to pick up her daughter.

She did not report the incident to either her mother or her father. She did not tell her husband when she returned home later that night because they were having marital problems.

Save Your Life

The next morning, RI was working out at the gym. Her friend, Eddie Currie, observed that RI was not her usual self. RI and Currie were very good friends, but were not romantically involved.

The two went to Currie's apartment where she told him that the defendant sexually assaulted her. Currie suggested that she report the assault to the police and seek counseling. On May 5, 1998, the next day, RI visited the Rape Crisis Center. On May 18, 1998, RI reported the sexual assault to Police.

On July 17, 2001, the jury convicted the defendant of counts one and two (second-degree sexual assault) and acquitted him of count three (fourth-degree criminal sexual contact).

My reading friends, this was not the end. More was to come. You see, a juror had been discharged. He was a Mason and reported he could not impartially judge the defendant who was wearing a Mason emblem pin in court.

After his conviction, the defendant used this to petition the Appeals Court. Lo and behold, his conviction was thrown out.

We return to the past. Below is the ruling of the Appeals Court.

We conclude that the trial court committed reversible error in its failure to declare a mistrial after properly discharging Juror Number 4.

A New Start in Texas

New Jersey was no longer my home. No way could I feel safe in the state where I had been frequently and viciously violated.

There were days when my heart slammed my chest, and panic overwhelmed me. I could not live like that.

I took my youngest child and moved as far away as I could get without leaving the U.S., relocating to Texas.

I am not sure that all of my family and friends understood, but I prayed that they would.

I took the seeds of strength that I had felt with Cynthia and Eddie, strength that I had glimpsed during the trial, and set off on a new journey toward self-discovery, again. I had a long way to go before I could embrace wellness.

Once more, vigorous feminine fitness became essential to my sense of independence, and it aided in protection of my daughter in our new homeland, Texas. I became a fitness instructor.

Though I had a new life, I kept in touch with loved ones, and even special acquaintances I met when I was in group counseling sessions in New Jersey. I wrote an article for the group's newsletter and sent it to be published.

The writing described my turmoil and, in the midst of my angst, an evolving spirituality. In the next chapter you will find a revised version of the article.

Save Your Life

When I reread it to include it in this book, I suddenly recalled long-buried details of the train wreck that was my life. The revision following is edited to protect loved ones who might not be willing to publicly relive a painful past.

Newsworthy From The Heart Of Texas
by Rashidah Id-Deen

My profound journey to Self-Discovery began on December 1, 2000. It's now February, 2001. Let me briefly give you some of the basic ingredients of this "bittersweet mixture" called Rashidah.

I am an African American woman in her late forties. This journey of Self-Discovery was provoked by the last three years of my life in which I was sexually assaulted–I am still awaiting trial–and had two car accidents, the second of which was so severe, it was written in the Courier newspaper.

I realize that my experiences are not unique by any means, however it's all about how we are equipped or choose to deal with our particular challenges that make them unique in that sense.

The culmination of all this put me under a doctor's care and caused as well an emotional and mental breakdown, which placed me in counseling.

Given the fact that my marriage wasn't solid to begin with, it stands to reason that the sexual assault was far too much for the marriage to withstand. So, I am left to deal with this alone, along with all of the ramifications and consequences that it brings.

My world had crashed, or so I thought. Even being a God-fearing woman didn't prevent me from being suicidal.

Save Your Life

Feeling totally depleted, defeated and devastated, I not only called on my Lord, I literally cried and begged OH GOD-PLEASE HELP ME!

Another person caught up in my turmoil was the youngest of my six children: my eleven-year-old daughter. As I became weaker in spirit and body, I noticed that she attempted at her tender age to become my caregiver. That broke what was left of my heart.

I didn't want her to become a casualty of my anguish. So, here I was no good to myself, not to mention my children, my grandchildren, my parents and the WORLD!!!

I felt like a complete failure. Worthless, useless, just taking up space and not even doing a decent job at that. I was totally stripped of my self-respect and dignity.

Suicide became a pleasant afterthought. Sometimes we have to be totally stripped of everything in order to experience a rebirth and transformation.

I then realized that the place, the space and the environment which I occupied had become toxic and polluted. The impact that this was having on me was that similar to QUICKSAND.

I had to change my soil. So, on December 1, 2000 with God's blessing, I embarked upon my journey of Self-Discovery. I moved to Texas with very little money and what seemed to be by conventional standards, no marketable job skills. However, with barely the basic material necessities, I have acquired more than I have ever had in my entire life.

Although I left a toxic environment, I also left an environment of lifetime comforts, family and friends. Leaving my parents who are up in age and my children (except for my youngest of course who is with me), was one of the hardest thing I have ever had to do.

I realize now that everything happens for a reason. But God in His infinite wisdom gives us choices. Depending on our choices, we can either gain closeness or be led astray.

Leaving "home" as I knew it truly brought me home. Home to God and myself.

I've now changed how I internally dialogue with myself. I no longer say, when something bad happens to me, why am I being punished?

Rather I choose to tell myself God is not finished with me yet! I am a work in progress and I choose to be fortified by God.

As a result of my changed thinking I have become a more spiritual being as opposed to religious. Religion for me deals with the external and ritualistic factors that one adheres to according to their faith, i.e. day of Congregational worship, garment of attire for worship, etc. All of this is important, but spiritual awareness goes beyond mass.

Spirituality is a 24-7, 365-day connection with our Lord regardless of a specific day of the week or place.

Save Your Life

I would like to share with my sisters from "Something For You," with God's will and permission, a periodic update and chronicle of my continued journey. This will allow me to have a voice and input into the group although I'm not there.

Hopefully, I can be a vehicle by which shared experiences spark healing conversations amongst group members or at the very least promote individual introspection. In your responses to me, please know that I welcome all comments and/or suggestions. May God remain with each and every one of us!

Peace & Blessings,
Rashidah

Rashidah Id-Deen

Just Proportions, a 2011 View

Celebration~

Recognition of my spiritual awareness in the newsletter was a celebration, and the contrasting balance it provided against the turmoil was much needed joy midst sorrows. God blessed me to discover that even with all my human weaknesses and ugliness exposed, I was spiritually growing strong and beautiful.

P#428324

The man who attacked me was now celebrated by his supporters, walking around, free in New Jersey. I was struggling to break free of fear and shame in Dallas, Texas, my new home.

My youngest child, my precious daughter was with me. For my sake, for my daughter, for the safety of women in New Jersey, I refused to give up on seeing this man imprisoned behind bars.

I insisted on another trial.

I got it in 2005.

And I won!

P#428324

It was a victory for all women when P#428324 was behind bars. This prison number was his new identity. No distinguished honor came with his name on an inmate roll, or with the number emblazoned on his institutional shirt.

I rejoiced, but I also suffered post-traumatic stress disorder.

Like veterans of war, I struggled to recover. Memories of the childhood and adult assaults trapped me in an indescribable hell.

After I won, I thought that long fought war was done. I was to find out how wrong I was.

The Year 2005~
New Trial

P#428324 was behind bars.
P#428324 was not sexually assaulting women.

My heart took hold of joy, squeezed it, tried to nourish my soul with it–used the victory to attempt hurdling over all obstacles encountered by any single mother in a new place.

I was hit by an 18-wheeler tractor trailer–on the driver's side of my little 1999 Toyota Tercel. It went airborne with me in it, over an embankment.

I sometimes picture that–wonder how it looked when others saw me flying through the air in my crushed Tercel.

Thank God, my daughter was not with me.

Now, by all visual and logical accounts, I should have been dead. Anything that does not kill us…

At a Texas hospital, in a rush of activity, medical magicians hooked me to webs of wires feeding beeping machines. They hooked me to tubes that kept me alive.

Doctors checked for internal bleeding. They discovered something else, something *suspicious*, when they looked at my X-ray and MRI images.

After my magicians patched me, they advised, "See your private care physician!"

Save Your Life

I followed that advice. My private care physician told me this: "There's a *growth* on your left kidney. We need to assess and evaluate immediately."

That growth turned out to be kidney cancer: Renal cell carcinoma.

I urgently needed surgery.

Cancer?!

Surgery?!

What new nightmare is this?!

Am I going to die? What will happen to my children?!

And of course, I asked the million-dollar question.

Why me?!

I had the surgery.

Later, I was informed that doctors had believed they could remove the tumor and save my left kidney. However, once inside, surgeons discovered that the tumor was bigger than previously thought. It had wrapped itself around the kidney. They had no choice but to remove it.

This news was not my biggest post-surgery surprise.

My primary surgeon informed me that he had removed the kidney *just in time.*

Just...in...time?

He explained: the accident saved my life.

You see, after I survived what should have killed me, doctors ran tests–of course–to determine what damage the accident caused. That's when they spotted the malignant growth wrapped around my kidney and recommended I see a private doctor.

I had followed that advice.

A freak accident that should have ended my life saved it.

What a profound *in-touch-with-God* moment this was for me–a spiritually enlightening *Aha* moment. It spoke directly to my existence, at that exact time, and to what was still waiting over a hill I had to climb.

Four months later, I got a call from New Jersey. It was the Union County Prosecutor, Ms. Daria Smith.

She stated that P#428324–*remember him?*–had been granted a retrial.

I felt the wind go out of my lungs.

She asked, "What do you want to do?"

Daria explained: If I chose not to go to trial again, which she would completely understand, she wanted me to be clear about the fact that the offender would be released, and released without any criminal record of the crime.

Daria understood how difficult it was for any woman to go through one trial, let alone consider having to go through the process again.

She attempted to comfort me with the fact that he had already served four years.

That was not enough for me.

I knew I had to fight this war to the end. I informed Daria that I was still recovering from kidney cancer surgery, but at this point, I felt that fighting to keep that rapist where he belonged was something I had to do.

Against my doctor's advice and my family's wishes, I pursued yet another trial.

During this trial, I thought a lot about the accident and how it saved my life. I played it over and over again in my head throughout the trial.

One of my favorite affirmations is this: *Everything is possible with God, and nothing is possible without Him.*

One arduous trial day, I was on the stand for about two hours giving testimony against the prisoner who had hired a good lawyer to go free. Finally, the judge called for a recess.

The defense attorney strode with purpose over to the prosecution table. For several intense minutes, he spoke to my attorney.

It turned out that the defense attorney saw and heard power in my TRUTH. He advised his client to strike a deal immediately.

I refused the deal. We continued the trial.

At the end of the first day of this 2005 trial, the man who assaulted me in 1998, the convicted sex offender who had petitioned the courts for a new trial advised his defense attorney that he wanted to plead guilty.

PLEAD GUILTY?!

He was told that if he were found guilty, he would start serving time all over again.

He was found guilty!

Some Special Childhood Memories, Too

Some special, loving moments with my childhood family were integral parts of my life. I am a product of the good times, too. I record them here.

My mother's singing: Mama often shared fond memories with the family of being in her high school chorus, and of the group winning the state choral championship. When she regaled us, she would sing a few of the songs.

Mama has a beautiful singing voice. I believe that's where my brother got his gifted voice.

My mother was an only child. I remember how she lovingly took care of her mother, my Grandma Gin (Virginia) and I remember thinking I wanted to have a tender, honorable relationship like that with my own mother.

I was very emotionally close to my Grandma Gin, though she wasn't physically present a lot. Now, Grandma Eula really helped to raise us and I will always appreciate her. However, the special closeness I felt with Grandma Gin was apparent to everyone in the family, and the feeling was obviously mutual.

Both my Grandmas have since passed. I think about them and pray for them often.

My daddy was and is a very disciplined man. For the most part, he did not interact with his children much during our early years; but, we would often overhear him sharing jokes with adult family members. We so enjoyed hearing laughter emanate from our "so serious" dad.

My sister and best friend, Sakinah, always appeared to possess a stronger sense of self than I did growing up, even though I'm the oldest. She was daring and tomboyish, and didn't care what anyone thought about her breaking the so called "feminine stereotype." I was the very girly girl; she was and is the very opposite.

My sister never had any biological children of her own. However, my children and grandchildren are HER children as well. She co-mothered each and every one of them from the time they were born, and we ALWAYS acknowledge her on Mother's Day.

Sakinah has a great sense of humor, and is very smart. She graduated from NYU with a B.A. in journalism.

My brother, Tariq, is the bona-fide comedian of the family. Hm-m-m, which reminds me of those times Dad laughed and joked, among adults, with a heartiness that spread cheer to us all. Tariq's impressive voice can easily be compared to that of the late, great Luther Vandross. Tariq does not have children.

I believe that the glories and the battles of my childhood were all in preparation for my passion: Helping Others. I am dedicated to the mission of navigating desperate souls through dark passages in their lives while helping them stay connected to our Most Powerful Source: The Sovereign, The Holy One, The Source of Peace and Perfection, and the Guardian of

Rashidah Id-Deen

Faith, GOD. With HIM everything IS possible, and without HIM nothing is!!!

Letter to My Children

It is time to pay tribute to six amazing people who were essential in saving my life. God blessed me to know them as my children.

Ayesha, Rahjan, Nadiyah, Rasul, Qasim & Amani:
Following is a letter to all of you.

Dear Beloveds,

Please know that I am so tremendously honored to be your mother. In you, I behold six beautiful, diversely gifted individuals. Your names announce the highest hopes for you.

Here, I record your names' meanings, and do so in your birth order, oldest to youngest. Of course, you already know what follows.

Ayesha	*Prosperous*; *Not dying*
Rahjan	*Seeker of Knowledge*
Nadiyah	*Lively*; *Pretty*;
	Fresh as a flower with morning dew
Rasul	*Messenger*
Qasim	*Undivisable; Oneness*
Amani	*Great Aspirations and Wishes*

Each of you is inimitable.
I treasure you.

Additionally in each of you,
two of your qualities that I see as excellence
and that bring me joy are –

Ayesha	*VERY SMART and Very Reserved*
Rahjan	*HARD-WORKING and Humorous*
Nadiyah	*STRONG-WILLED and Motherly*
Rasul	*DARING and Adventurous*
Qasim	*FUNNY and Easy-going*
Amani	*SPIRITUALLY CONSCIOUS and Very Nurturing*

Now, it is my privilege to also see manifested in the flesh six different physical, emotional and spiritual personalities of myself. For better or worse, I see how the totality of my life has impacted yours.

Before becoming your mother, I was just a young girl, a young confused and frightened girl. This same confused and frightened girl became your mother.

When a person has been consistently abused without receiving emotional help and/or a deeper understanding of what has transpired in your soul from such devastating abuse, there is no buffer to keep it from permeating all aspects of your life, especially motherhood. Abuse negatively colors every thought process you possess.

Save Your Life

But, as children it was not your responsibility to be aware of or responsible for the healing of your parents. You, my children, expected and deserved to have a happy, healthy, and well-adjusted mother.

Despite how hard I tried to mask the pain and present an image contrary to the reality of my troubled being, I was unsuccessful. I deeply regret and apologize for not being "present" emotionally to fulfill your needs.

I did however provide all the physical necessities to the best of my ability and feel I did an adequate job at that as a single parent. But, emotionally I was out of balance, confused, scared, ashamed, and I lacked a sense of self-worth.

I, as a mother, understood that I was your introduction to the world and I wanted it to be far better than the reality of my world.

Each of you manifests a particular aspect of the pathology of my abuse. I am sorry for the negative emotional impact it has had on each of your lives in uniquely different ways.

It is my prayer and intention in writing this book to "save our lives, and not our image." To expose and declare that as of this day, the secrecy, hypocrisy and family curse will be obliterated.

I sincerely ask each of you to forgive me, and I ask that you forgive yourselves for whatever negative responses and reactions my emotional dysfunction provoked in you.

Rashidah Id-Deen

Forgive, forgive, forgive!

No longer allow pointing a finger of blame to deflect chances for your healing. Blame won't delete shame, and shame just produces more of the same—more shame.

All of you are exceptionally stronger than you even know. Allow that strength to come to the front and center, to stand up and declare a new course of action and reactions in your lives.

It all begins with choosing a new and productive thought pattern. Yes it's a process, but you first must be willing to establish a "conscious intent," know that your future well-being depends on it, and that you and your own families deserve it.

Unfortunately, there are no "do-overs" in real life. If I could change the past, I would have told you when you were all younger *how much I love you*, and not expect that somehow automatically you would have known or felt it just because I was biologically your mother.

I would have told and shown you then that no matter what happens to us, it is what is happening inside of us that really determines the status and quality of our lives.

I would also have told you about the power of forgiveness and that it is a gift we give to ourselves, and does not mean that we accept or condone the inappropriate behavior or abuse. We simply and powerfully remove and disconnect ourselves from any further attachment or association to it.

Save Your Life

I would have smiled more. I don't think all of you remember me smiling. I don't.

I would have been more present in the many milestones of your growing up years and created more moments of celebration.

I would have told you back then that
the power of love, that of self-love particularly,
is the most powerful human force of all.

I beg each of you to please not make any or the same mistakes I have made with myself and with you, my wonderful children.

It's not too late because with every God-given breath, He allows us another opportunity and chance to make a better choice than the one before. Praise Him, thank Him and always turn and rely on Him for He is always there. As one of you once said to me "when you find yourself removed from God, ask yourself who moved?"

Today is a new day and a new chapter for our family. We can collectively and individually establish conscious awareness of our need to heal and commit our intention to genuinely healing.

I love each of you more than you will ever know or words can express. It can be greater later. Believe it, seek it and so it is!

My Love Always,
Mom

The Power of Self~Love

The power of love, that of self-love particularly, is the most powerful human force of all.

Love in all its magnificence and power originated with God! When we were created, God wanted all of us to love ourselves, and others, as He loves us~with righteousness and honor, purity and grace, respect and dignity, power and majesty.

Self-love incorporates all of these.

It is not selfish to honor God's gift of life in the flesh. It is a tribute to The Sovereign.

When we become selfish, which is different from self-loving, we are farthest away from God's intention for us. Selfishness lacks righteousness and honor, purity and grace, respect and dignity, power and majesty.

We grow strongest when we embrace authentic love and share it. We grow weakest when we deny, abuse, or attempt to corrupt it. These lessons, I had to learn the hard way.

Through travail and life trials, and with the warm embrace of friends and family, God directed my path to a heightened spiritual joy. Thank you, God.

I share this joy with my current husband, Jamil, our beloved family and friends, and all who insist on living in spiritual enlightenment.

Save Your Life

I finally understand that it is more than merely alright to love and protect myself, it is intended that I do so. This is following God's will.

My name *Rashidah* means *One who follows the Right Guide or Conscious*. The meaning of *Id-Deen* is *of the Faith, the Religion*.

I am finally ready to allow and whole-heartedly accept God's intent for me ~ that I love myself with righteousness and honor, purity and grace, respect and dignity, power and majesty.

Are you ready to accept this intent for you?

When we learn to love ourselves, we are then ready to offer others love at its best.

Just Proportions Foundation and Collaborations

JUST PROPORTIONS Foundation is my 501 (c)(3) tax exempt non-profit organization, founded in 2005 for survivors of domestic violence and sexual abuse. The mission is to serve as a resource facility for women, providing education, peer counseling and support for survivors of domestic violence and sexual abuse. We strive to connect with women on every level as they aspire for personal growth.

The vision of JUST PROPORTIONS is to identify and address psychological and behavioral patterns that perpetuate cycles of domestic violence and sexual abuse. In *caring for ourselves*, we can achieve healthy relationships with our family, friends and loved ones.

Collaboration among agencies that provide quality care services for women and children survivors of assault is vital. I have served as Hotline Volunteer and Courtroom Advocate for Brighter Tomorrows, a Texas agency that advocates for survivors of violence and sexual abuse.

I was a Guest Speaker and Facilitator of a national conference workshop for Health of Women & Girls (HoW-G1), also in Texas. We worked to build a bridge of help leading to healthier futures for all girls and women.

JUST PROPORTIONS FOUNDATION can serve as a beacon of hope for the end of sexual assault and

Save Your Life

domestic violence. The day I, the FOUNDATION's Founder, heard the sexual offender who violated me plead guilty after lying for years was the day I realized my calling. There are others survivors out here needing help and I am going to provide it. I have much work to do.

Contemporary Guide for Survivors of Assault
Introduction

The *Contemporary Guide for Survivors of Assault* is for anyone who is experiencing or has experienced abuse and is seeking empowerment. I refer to it as contemporary to remind us that in this age of global information sharing, we can disseminate life-saving knowledge quicker and more efficiently than ever before.

The Internet, with a world of social interface networks, connects us–for better or worse. It is my privilege to connect with you here. We can also reach each other through blogs, YouTube, virtual Internet worlds, and more electronic means than I can name.

Now, we begin your *Save Your Life* journey in this guide.

The *Contemporary Guide* is divided into four parts. In Part 1, we will give *knowledge* power to save our lives. We will use what I call Knowledge Points or KPs to examine sexual assault or abuse and domestic violence.

A KP is my reference to vital information that we need to know. After we know it, we need to apply it.

In Part 2, you have a personal *Save My Life* worksheet, preceded by *Save My Life* worksheet preparation. Exercises can walk you through examining abuse or assaults in your life in order to take steps toward healing. We must know what is broken before we can mend it.

Part 3 is a place and space to celebrate being you! You are divinely designed. Express joy and give yourself some love!

Part 4 is a directory of counseling and referral services. When we need help, we must know who to call and where to go. This directory can serve as a valuable starting point.

Contemporary Guide for Survivors of Assault~
Part 1: Knowledge is Power

The first Knowledge Point is this: There is something uniquely special about you. Repeat it, believe it, and feel it!

Your purpose on this earth has a divine design. You deserve to love and be loved ~ with righteousness and honor, purity and grace, respect and dignity, power and majesty.

If you are offered love that is embedded in secrecy and shame, something is wrong. You might even ask–*is it love?*

Second Knowledge Point: Recovery from any type of toxicity does not guarantee us delivery from the pangs of life. We do not suddenly become immune to hunger, anger, loneliness, or desolate tiredness.

When we are in a healthy stage of recovery, our awareness helps us identify our joys in addition to sorrows. We see the balance; we see the just proportions, and we celebrate our lives.

I come to you with Knowledge Points gained the hard way, experience. It has earned me a Ph.D. in Life.

I am not a licensed professional counselor, though I have been trained in peer counseling. If you have been abused, I suggest that in addition to self-help you seek professional guidance. I did.

Let's look at some additional Knowledge Points, KPs.

Save Your Life

KP: It is urgent that you seek and maintain personal safety if your life is in danger. If you have children, please recognize that you cannot fully protect them until you can protect yourself. If they are in danger, it is urgent that you get them to safety. There are shelters that will house you and your children.

KP: You can't teach what you don't know. Do you know what love is? Do you love yourself? Now, would be a good time to define love and self-love. Once you know, you can teach others, especially your children. Please re-read *The Power of Self~Love*, which is found earlier in this book.

Now, we are ready to discuss KPs, definitions, and descriptions of sexual assault or abuse, although most of us are already too aware of what they are.

Sexual Assault or Abuse

Knowledge Point: Sexual assault or abuse is the use of physical, mental, emotional and/or psychological power to do any of the following:

> Rape
> Attempt to Rape
> Have Intercourse
> Perform Vaginal, Anal, or Oral Sex
> Inappropriately Touch
> Molest a Child
> Engage in Incest.

Rashidah Id-Deen

The person committing the sexual assault, the perpetrator, could be someone we trust or even love–a family member, friend, or authority figure, and could be male or female.

The assault can start with or include a smile and soft touch. Because many of us are starved for love and attention, the initial contact might feel good–this can sometimes makes it hard to identify the violation–but, eventually that special sense of right and wrong kicks in. Of course, with a very young child or a psychologically challenged person, that sense might not be significantly developed.

It is always the perpetrator's responsibility to restrain himself or herself, but in real life sexual abuse, that is not happening. We, the survivors, are left picking up the pieces of someone else's sickness.

The perpetrator could also be a stranger. He or she could be aggressive or appear friendly and inviting.

Sexual assault of any kind is malevolent. There is no excuse to justify it. There may be plenty of insights that help us understand it, but there is NO ACCEPTABLE EXCUSE.

Below is information about sexual assault provided by organizations dedicated to educating and alerting the public. This information is free in literature and on the Web. In later sections of this guide, you will find exercises designed just for you–to help you take steps toward saving your life and sanity.

Save Your Life

An American is sexually assaulted every two and a half minutes. *(RAINN, 2007)*

One in six American women has been the victim of attempted or completed rape. *(RAINN, 2007)*

Approximately 44% of rape victims are under the age of 18; about 15% are under the age of 12. *(RAINN, 2007)*

Youths 12-17 are two to three times more likely to be sexually assaulted than adults. *(National Crime Victimization Survey, 2000)*

Approximately 10% of sexual assault victims are men. *(RAINN, 2007)*

73% of rape victims know their assailant [they are NOT a stranger]. *(National Crime Victimization Survey, 2005)*

Nearly 7.8 million women have been raped by an intimate partner at some point in their lives. *(Costs of Intimate Partner Violence Against Women in the United States. 2003)*

Note: RAINN stands for Rape, Abuse & Incest National Network.

Rashidah Id-Deen

Domestic Violence

Here, we will examine Knowledge Points/KPs, definitions, and descriptions of domestic violence.

KP: Domestic violence turns homes into battlefields. It is physical, mental, and emotional assault within a family system. Often, domestic violence travels across generations, but not always.

Violators have no sincere respect for the sanctity of home, family, or childhood. Often, violators have no or little respect for themselves, and mask self-hatred with aggression and victimization of others.

Symptoms of domestic violence can manifest in any family member as one or more of the traits below. This list is not exhaustive. You may be able to add some of your own.

    Depression
    Unresolved Anger
    Inability to Cope With Life
    Hopelessness
    Crisis-oriented
    Hypervigilance
        (Anxious, Waiting
      for Next Crisis)
    Fear of Abandonment
    Fear of Engulfment
    Alcoholism
    Drug Addiction
    Perfectionism

Save Your Life

Overachievement
Comic Response to Tragedy

Domestic violence knows no boundaries or class distinction. It can happen in homes of the rich or poor.

It cuts across all religious denominations: Protestant, Catholic, Islam, or any other. It can happen in a family of any nationality–African-American, Asian, European-American, Hispanic, and others.

Below are some reports on domestic violence. This information is free in literature and on the Web. In later sections of this guide, you will find exercises designed just for you–to help you take steps toward saving your life and sanity.

There are 16,800 homicides and $2.2 million (medically treated) injuries due to intimate partner violence annually, which costs $37 billion. *(The Cost of Violence in the United States. Centers for Disease Control and Prevention, National Centers for Injury Prevention and Control. Atlanta, GA., 2007)*

85% of domestic violence victims are women. *(Bureau of Justice Statistics Crime Data Brief, Intimate Partner Violence, 1993-2001, February 2003)*

An estimated 1.3 million women are victims of physical assault by an intimate partner each year. *(Costs of*

Rashidah Id-Deen

Intimate Partner Violence Against Women in the United States. Centers for Disease Control and Prevention, National Centers for Injury Prevention and Control. Atlanta, GA., 2003)

Witnessing violence between one's parents or caretakers is the strongest risk factor of transmitting violent behavior from one generation to the next. *(Frieze, I.H., Browne, A., 1989) Violence in Marriage. In L.E. Ohlin & M. H. Tonry, Family Violence. Chicago, IL: University of Chicago Press. Break the Cycle, 2006)*

One in every four women will experience domestic violence in her lifetime. *(Tjaden, Patricia & Thoennes, Nancy. National Institute of Justice and the Centers of Disease Control and Prevention, "Extent, Nature and Consequences of Intimate Partner Violence: Findings from the National Violence Against Women Survey," 2000; Sara Glazer, "Violence, Against Women" CO Researcher, Congressional Quarterly, Inc., Volume 3, Number 8, February, 1993, p. 171; The Centers for Disease Control and Prevention and The National Institute of Justice, Extent, Nature, and Consequences of Intimate Partner Violence, July 2000)*

Nearly three out of four (74%) of Americans personally know someone who is or has been a victim of domestic violence. 30% of Americans say they know a woman who has been physically abused by her husband or boyfriend in the past year. *(Allstate Foundation National Poll on Domestic Violence, 2006. Lieberman Research Inc., Tracking Survey conducted for The Advertising Council and the Family Violence Prevention Fund, July – October 1996)*

Contemporary Guide for Survivors of Assault~
Part 2: Save My Life Worksheet Preparation;
Save My Life Worksheet

It is a normal human reaction to avoid pain. Feeling it is not on our "to do" lists; but sometimes, we must experience pain while identifying the source of it.

In this part of the *Contemporary Guide*, I give you worksheets to help you pinpoint facts you buried in order to get on with your life. The problem is that sometimes we reach a point where we can't just get on with it.

Work, taking care of the kids, even making love can seem like monumental tasks. We get through them without a real sense of joy.

We might even have become numb to our pain for such a long time, we don't even think we have problems. Perhaps, our unidentified or identified pain spills over into the lives of loved ones who act out because they feel neglected, unwanted, even unloved.

But, as long as our lives appear to be running smoothly, or semi-smoothly, we see no reason to delve into the murky past. The deep delve often becomes a valuable tool only when we know we need to unearth trauma sources in order to root out the resulting pain.

Have an honest talk with yourself. Identify the abuse that keeps you held back, keeps you from being the best that you can be.

Save Your Life

I confronted personal abuse with the aid of a counselor. I suggest that you also seek professional assistance as you use this guide; but, you can choose to work it in complete privacy–for your eyes only. When you talk to yourself, make sure you listen.

Additionally, if I were you, I would turn to God for love and guidance before starting any in-depth inspection of trauma in my life.

Rashidah Id-Deen

Pre-Guide Exercise:
Create a Mental Oasis ~
Picture Yourself in a Safe Place

Imagine yourself in a safe place.
It can be indoors or outdoors.
This is your world.
Fill it with sights, sounds, smells, tastes that make you feel happy.
Remove sights, sounds, smells, tastes that make you unhappy.
Now, how does it feel?
What colors surround you?
Is there music?
If yes, what music?
Make yourself happy here.
While working the exercises of this guide, if you ever need a mental oasis, come back here.

Save Your Life

Save My Life Worksheet

(You might need additional sheets of paper.)

1. **What abuse/assault did I experience?**

   _____
   _____
   _____

2. **Who assaulted me?**

   _____
   _____
   _____

3. **How old was I?**

   _____

4. **What happened and where did it happen?**

   _____
   _____
   _____
   _____

5. **What did I feel at first when I was assaulted? (Bodily Sensations and Emotions)**

_____

_____

_____

_____

_____

6. **What did I feel later (hours, days, weeks, months and/or years later? (Bodily Sensations and Emotions)**
   (You might want to discuss this with a professional counselor.)

_____

_____

_____

_____

_____

7. **Was I assaulted more than once?**

_____

_____

_____

8. **How did the assault(s) change me?**

   _____
   _____
   _____
   _____
   _____

9. **How did the person who assaulted me respond afterwards?**

   _____
   _____

10. **Am I in danger physically or psychologically? If yes, how?**

    _____
    _____
    _____
    _____
    _____
    _____

11. **Whom can I call or talk to if I am in danger? What are the related phone numbers, addresses, or e-mail addresses?**

_____
_____
_____
_____
_____
_____
_____
_____
_____

12. **What will I say?**

_____
_____
_____
_____
_____

13. **Am I willing to put prayer with appropriate action that will help me to be and feel safe?**

14. **Am I ready to grieve my loss of whatever was taken from me (personal ownership of my body, innocence, virginity, dignity, sense of self, self-love, _____)?** Grief is a normal reaction to loss of something important to us.

15. **Am I already grieving?**

16. **In what stage of grief am I?**
    The stages of grief discussed in this book are Denial, Anger, Bargaining, Depression and Acceptance. The stages may take place in a different order. See grief stage examples or descriptions below.

17. **Denial? What do I see or feel that indicates I am in denial?**
Example: "No, it really didn't happen."

_____
_____
_____

18. **Anger? What do I see or feel that indicates I am angry?** Description: Rage or oppositional behavior can be easy to identify as anger, but sarcasm or passive-aggressive behavior are sometimes the ways anger surfaces.

_____
_____
_____

19. **Bargaining? What do I see or feel that indicates I am bargaining?**
Example: "God, if you do ..., I will ..."

_____
_____
_____

20. **Depression? What do I see or feel that indicates I am depressed?**

Description: Depression is a state of feeling down or sad. Some people just feel numb.

_____

_____

_____

21. **Acceptance? What do I see or feel that indicates I am in acceptance?**
Example: "This is what happened. I hate that it did, but it happened."

_____

_____

_____

22. **Am I experiencing more than 1 stage of grief?**

_____

_____

_____

23. **After grieving, when I start to heal, am I willing to celebrate the good in my life?**

_____

_____

_____

24. **What would I like to do to celebrate? (Sing, dance, draw, write poetry, write my own book, smile, laugh or whatever other healthy thing my heart desires!)**

_____
_____
_____

Contemporary Guide for Survivors of Assault~
Part 3: My Space~
Celebration of My Life

Do you like to draw or write poetry? Maybe you have seen others expressing these talents and wondered if you could. Now is the time, here in your own personal guidebook, to pick up a pencil and draw a picture celebrating you and your life or to write poetry.

The goal here is not perfection. It is something far more important. The goal is to celebrate You! Show yourself some love!

This space isn't big enough? Oh! Get more paper!

 My Drawing

Rashidah Id-Deen

My Poetry

_____

_____
_____
_____
_____
_____
_____
_____
_____
_____
_____
_____
_____
_____
_____
_____
_____
_____
_____
_____

Contemporary Guide for Survivors of Assault~ Part 4: Directory for Counseling and Referral Services

Professional counseling can be a lifeline when we need it. There are many diverse services available. Hotlines offer immediate phone responses to urgent care needs. Many also provide phone numbers and locations of local counseling agencies where you can meet face-to-face with trained caregivers.

Below is a directory to locate counseling services for a variety of needs including Domestic Violence and Rape Trauma (Sexual Assault). The information is online, free of charge and the public is given permission to reprint without a fee.

Domestic Violence

National Domestic Violence Hotline: 800-799-SAFE 800-799-7233 and 800-787-3224 (TTY).

24-hour-a-day hotline, Provides crisis intervention and referrals to local services and shelters for victims of partner or spousal abuse. English and Spanish speaking advocates are available 24 hours a day, seven days a week. Staffed by trained volunteers who are ready to connect people with emergency help in their own communities, including emergency services and shelters.

The staff can also provide information and referrals for a variety of non-emergency services, including counseling for adults and children, and assistance in reporting abuse. They have an extensive database of domestic violence treatment providers in all US states and territories. Many staff members speak languages besides English, and they have 24-hour access to translators for approximately 150 languages. For the hearing impaired, there is a TTY number. This is a great resource for anyone--man, woman or child--who is experiencing or has experienced domestic violence or abuse, or who suspects that someone they know is being abused.

HIV/AIDS/Sexually Transmitted Diseases

The CDC (Center for Disease Control) National Prevention Information Network: 800-458-5231 9AM-6PM Mon-Fri includes info on new medicines, treatment trials, HIV & AIDS, with info specialists avail. to answer questions; also at www.CDCNAC.org (CDC National Aids Clearinghouse)

National AIDS Hotline: 800-342-AIDS (2437)

Information and referrals to local hotlines, testing centers, and counseling. Open 24 hours, seven days a week.

Save Your Life

AIDS Hotline in Spanish: 800-344-SIDA (7432) Open 8 a.m. to 2 a.m. Eastern Standard Time, seven days a week.

AIDS Hotline for the Hearing Impaired: 800-243-7889 (TDD) Open 10 a.m. to 10 p.m. Eastern Standard Time, Monday through Friday

National Sexually Transmitted Disease Hotline: 800-227-8922 Information and referrals to free and low-cost public clinics. Operators can answer general questions on prevention, symptoms, transmission and treatment of sexually transmitted diseases. Open 8 a.m. to 11 p.m. Eastern Standard Time, Monday through Friday.

Sexually Transmitted Disease & AIDS/HIV Information Hotline: 800-332-2437, TTY - 800-332-3889 (Ohio)

Parent Hotline

800-840-6537: Parent Hotline is a website dedicated to helping families who are in a crisis situation. It lists behaviors for parents to be aware of such as drug use and a questionnaire on if a child is in need of intervention.

Rape

Nationwide RAINN National Rape Crisis Hotline: 800-656-4673

Runaway/Exploited Children

Missing Children Network: 800-235-3535

Thursday's Child's National Youth Advocacy Hotline at 800-USA KIDS

National Hotline for Missing and Exploited Children: 800-843-5678

Operates a hotline for reporting missing children and sightings of missing children. Offers assistance to law enforcement agents. Hours of operation are 7:30 a.m.-11 p.m. Eastern Standard Time.

National Runaway Switchboard: 800-621-4000

Provides crisis intervention and travel assistance to runaways. Provides information and local referrals to adolescents and families. Gives referrals to shelters nationwide. Also relays messages to, or sets up conference calls with, parents at the request of the child. Operates 24 hours, seven days a week.

Child Find of America Hotline: 800-I-AM-LOST (426-5678)

Looks for missing and abducted children. Operators available 9 a.m. to 5 p.m. EST Monday-Friday.

Save Your Life

Voicemail on evenings and weekends with calls returned.

CONFIDENTIAL Runaway Hotline: 800-231-6946

Parent Abduction Hotline: 800-292-9688

Provides crisis mediation in parental abduction. Provides prevention information and referrals to local agencies. Operators available 9 a.m. to 5 p.m. EST Monday-Friday. Voicemail on evenings and weekends with calls returned.

Substance Abuse/Alcoholism

24/7 Drug and Alcohol Rehab Referral Service (Private, High End Facilities) 800-521-7128

24 Hour Drug Addiction Hotlines

Drug rehab referral services; includes large list of drug-specific helplines and hotlines.

24 Hour Alcohol Abuse Recovery Hotline

Alcohol rehab referral services; includes state and local hotline information and treatment center facility locator.
The Alcohol & Drug Addiction Resource Center
800 390 4056

Rashidah Id-Deen

Boys Town National Hotline 800-448-3000

National Drug Information Treatment and Referral Hotline: 800-662-HELP (4357)

Information, support, treatment options and referrals to local rehab centers for any drug or alcohol problem. Operates 24 hours, seven days a week.

National Cocaine Hotline: 800-COCAINE (262-2463)

Information, crisis intervention, and referrals to local rehab centers for all types of drug dependency. Operates 24 hours, seven days a week.

Al-ateen: 800-352-9996

Alcohol Abuse and Crisis Intervention: 800-234-0246

Alcohol and Drug Abuse Helpline and Treatment: 800-234-0420

Alcohol Hotline Support & Information: 800-331-2900

Save Your Life

Just Proportions Privilege

It has been a great honor to share parts of my life journey with you. If my disclosures have helped anyone, then *Save Your Life* has served its purpose.

It will be my privilege and challenge to allow the wellness principle of Just Proportions to continue manifesting in my life. From time to time, I will need to recreate healthy lifestyle balances. You might find a need to do the same.

At the end of this book, in an appendix, you will find pages for you to examine your thoughts and feelings regarding how you might have related to experiences I described. Were there times when you read passages that reminded you of your own life?

I would love to hear from you.
If you would like to contact me and share news of your experiences, please e-mail me at
justproportionsfoundation@yahoo.com
or visit my Website,
www.wix.com/justproportionsfound/Rashidah.

Peace, Joy, Blessings & Love,
Rashidah

Appendix

Save Your Life

Self-Reflection

1. What experiences in Rashidah's life reminded me of my own?

   _____
   _____
   _____

2. How did I feel when I read about the rape when she was twelve?

   _____
   _____
   _____

3. Has anything like that ever happened to me?

   _____
   _____
   _____

4. What did I think of the man who raped her when she was a girl?

   _____
   _____
   _____

5. What do I think should have happened to him?

   _____
   _____
   _____

6. Do I think counseling for a survivor of sexual assault would have helped Rashidah as a child?

_____
_____
_____

7. Where would I go if I needed this kind of counseling?

_____
_____
_____

8. Do I think Rashidah's assault experience as a girl influenced her choice of husbands as a woman?

_____
_____
_____

9. What are the reasons I answered as I did in number 8?

_____
_____
_____

10. Was I surprised to find out that one of her husbands had a problem with drugs?

_____
_____
_____

11. What are the reasons I answered as I did in number 10?

   _____
   _____
   _____

12. Was I surprised to find out that she was abused in her first marriage?

   _____
   _____
   _____

13. What are the reasons I answered as I did in number 12?

   _____
   _____
   _____

14. How did I react when Rashidah was sexually assaulted by the doctor?

   _____
   _____
   _____

15. What did I think of her friend, Eddie?

   _____
   _____
   _____

16. Would I have been that kind of friend?

   _____
   _____
   _____

17. What did I think of the trials?

18. Would I have pursued justice in court?

19. How did I react when I read that in the 2005 trial the sexual offender plead guilty?

20. What roles do I think physical illnesses played in Rashidah's life?

21. What was my reaction to her car crash?

22. What role did family play in Rashidah's life?

23. What was my least favorite part of this book?
_____
_____
_____

24. What was my favorite part of this book?
_____
_____
_____